Fort Loudoun Regional Library
718 George St.
Athens, Tenn. 37303

FOREWORD

"Frontiers of America" dramatizes some of the explorations and discoveries of real pioneers in simple, uncluttered text. America's spirit of adventure is seen in these early people who faced dangers and hardship blazing trails, pioneering new water routes, becoming Western heroes as well as legends, and building log forts and houses as they settled in the wilderness.

Although today's explorers and adventurers face different frontiers, the drive and spirit of these early pioneers in America's past still serve as an inspiration.

ABOUT THE AUTHOR

During her years as a teacher and reading consultant in elementary schools, Mrs. McCall developed a strong interest in the people whose pioneering spirit built our nation. When she turned to writing as a full-time occupation, this interest was the basis for much of her work. She is the author of many books and articles for children and adults, and co-author of elementary school social studies textbooks.

Frontiers of America

Cumberland Gap

AND TRAILS WEST

By Edith McCall

Pictures by Carol Rogers

CHILDRENS PRESS, CHICAGO

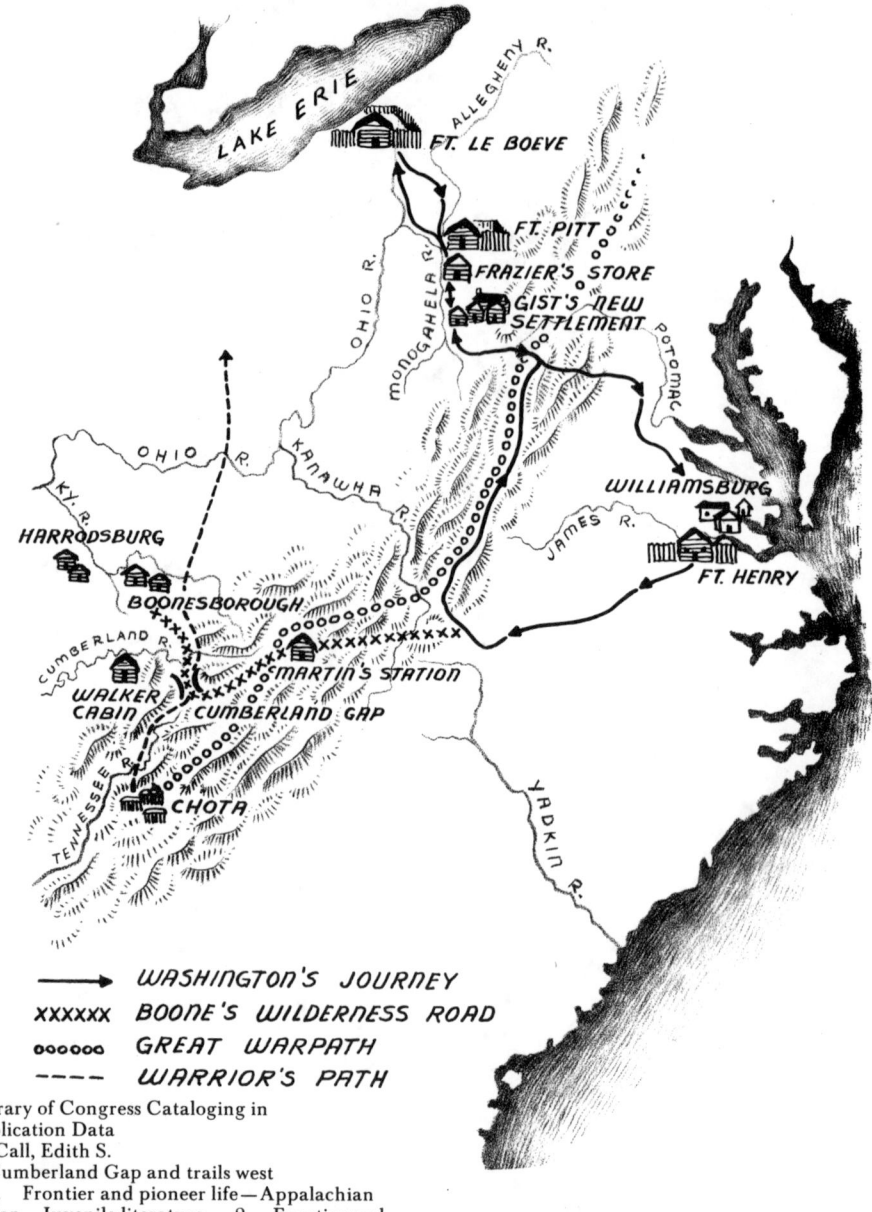

Library of Congress Cataloging in Publication Data
McCall, Edith S.
  Cumberland Gap and trails west
  1. Frontier and pioneer life—Appalachian region—Juvenile literature. 2. Frontier and pioneer life—Northwest, Old—Juvenile literature 3. Appalachian region—History—Juvenile literature. 4. Northwest, Old—History—To 1775—Juvenile literature.
  [1. Frontier and pioneer life. 2. Appalachian region—History] I. Rogers, Carol. II. Title.
  F106.M3   973.2   61-10102
  ISBN 0-516-03311-5

Cover photograph courtesy of James P. Rowan

New 1980 Edition
Copyright© 1961 by Regensteiner Publishing Enterprises, Inc.
All rights reserved. Published simultaneously in Canada.
Printed in the United States of America.
1 2 3 4 5 6 7 8 9 10 11 12 R 87 86 85 84 83 82 81 80

TRUE STORIES OF REAL MEN

THOMAS BATTS FINDS THE GREAT WARPATH.. 7

GABE ARTHUR WALKS THE WARRIORS' PATH.. 17

THOMAS WALKER FOLLOWS A BUFFALO TRACE 33

WASHINGTON AND THE FRENCH INDIAN...... 46

WASHINGTON AND THE WILD ALLEGHENY.... 66

PEDDLER WITH A PACK OF DREAMS.......... 77

BOONE'S LONG HUNT, BIG TROUBLE 86

BOONE STOPPED BY INDIANS................101

WILDERNESS ROAD............................113

THOMAS BATTS FINDS
THE GREAT WARPATH

It was a September day in Virginia, a long, long time ago. The United States of America was not yet a country. Where the nation would be in later years was almost all wilderness, except for a settled strip along the Atlantic Ocean.

There the colonies were, little villages near the mouths of the rivers, and a scattering of farms between them. There the people lived who had come, mostly from England, to find new homes in America.

Even then, in 1671, about sixty years after John Smith had helped get Virginia started at Jamestown, there was a western frontier. But it was less than a hundred miles from the Atlantic Ocean. There were a few forts on the frontier. They had been built because of the fur trading business. It had not taken the colonists long to learn that the Indians would bring them fine furs in trade for cheap cloth or knives or beads or tin whistles.

One of the forts was named Fort Henry. It stood

where Petersburg, Virginia, is today. The man in charge of Fort Henry was General Abraham Wood. Like many other men, General Wood looked often to the western wilderness and wondered what was there. But unlike most of the others, General Wood did something. He went exploring.

Each time he headed west, he found himself climbing hills that led only to higher hills.

Beyond the higher hills was a long, long ridge of mountains. The mountains rose like a great wall, running from Pennsylvania and New York in the north, to Georgia in the south. At first, the colonists thought they could find a river which cut through the mountains. Just the other side, they were sure, was the Great Western Sea, the Pacific Ocean. But all the rivers they followed came down to the Atlantic Ocean, and did not run west through the mountains.

"We will have to look for a river which starts just over the mountain ridge," they decided. "It will go to the Great Western Sea, and we can open a road to it. Then we will be able to trade with China."

There was still plenty of room between the mountain wall and the Atlantic Ocean. No one was crowded in the colonies, and there was still plenty of farm land to be cleared. But General Wood wanted to learn more about the land over the mountains. He wanted to find that river to the Western Sea.

On the first day of September in 1671, General Wood said good-by to a little group of five men on horseback. There was Captain Thomas Batts, leader of the group, Robert Fallam, young Thomas Wood and Jack Nason, who had been the general's servant for many years. The fifth man was an Appomatock Indian named Perecute. Perecute had lived at Fort Henry for years, and could speak English.

"Good luck, gentlemen!" General Wood said. "I wish I were young enough to go with you. Find that river to the Great Western Sea and we'll all be rich. The trade of the world will go through Fort Henry."

He watched the five riders until they disappeared from sight.

They found the traveling rough after the first few days. Poor Thomas Wood became sick and died in an Indian village.

Just before they crossed the mountain ridge, the traveling became too rough for the horses. They left the animals at an Indian village, and set out on foot for the rest of the trip up the mountains, with two Indians from the village to help carry their packs.

On the other side of the ridge, they began to pick their way down a hillside covered with trees, brush, vines and briers that made the going slow. Perecute climbed a tree and there, below him, was the shining ribbon of a river. They went on, as fast as the wilderness would let them, to follow the river that ran north and west.

They had been traveling two weeks and Captain Batts wanted to get to the river as quickly as possible. Near the river, they came upon a pathway through the brush.

"Fine!" Captain Batts said. "This is better."

But Perecute bent over to study the dusty trail.

The trail was old, and many, many moccasined feet had traveled it. Had some gone by in the hours just past?

"What do you make of it?" asked Captain Batts.

Perecute was not yet ready to say. He followed the trail a short way and then came back. He seemed satisfied with what he had learned.

"Moccasin prints tell of tribes that go northwest,

not long ago. We go northwest, too, and not meet them."

"Good," said Captain Batts. "The trail follows the river, and this will be easier than cutting our way through the wilderness. We'd better make camp now."

The two Indians from the mountain village came up to the place where Perecute and Jack Nason were clearing away brush for a camp site. They put down the packs and hurried to the trail to study it as Perecute had done. But, as they looked, they pointed at the footprints and talked excitedly.

"What are they saying?" asked Robert Fallam.

Perecute said, "They fear we will meet the enemy on this trail. It is the *Great Warpath,* and over it travel the war parties who come down from the north. The trail is many, many miles long, following the valley between the mountains we have crossed and those to the west. These two men do not want to go on."

"But we *must* go on!" Captain Batts said. "We came over the mountains to find a river to the Great Western Sea. That could be the river, just below us, but we must follow it farther to know. Tell them we

will pay them well, but we *must* go on."

The Indians finally agreed to go a little farther. In the next few days, the travelers saw open meadows, and fields where old, dry cornstalks stood. There were signs of many old campfires near the trail. Captain Batts asked Perecute more about this trail through the valley. Perecute had not traveled it himself, but he had heard of it. It led, at the south end, to an important Cherokee village, and at the north to the land of the Iroquois tribes.

Each day, the two Indians studied the trail closely. And each day, they were less willing to go on. Even Perecute began to talk of danger, and to ask that they turn back. The river was about to swing away from the trail, to wind between the mountains to the west.

"Masters," Perecute said. "There is evil beyond those mountains. We cannot go on."

Thomas Batts was disappointed. He was sure that he had seen ocean mists as he followed the river's winding path through his spy glass. He called Fallam to his side.

"Look yonder, Robert," he said. "See those white patches through the mists? I think they are sails.

The Great Western Sea must be just beyond that next ridge."

Fallam studied the patches of white through the glass. "Possibly, Thomas," he said. "But I think more likely they are white cliffs on the ocean's edge, like those back in England on the shore of the English Channel."

Both men were sure the river led to the sea. They made their way to the river's bank to study it more closely. They saw a wetness on the banks above the water line that showed the water had been higher. The rivers of Virginia went up and down each day with the ocean tides on the coastal plain where the colonies had been built. "Tidewater lands" they called them, because of the tides in the rivers.

"See the mark of high tide on the bank?" Captain Batts said. "That means we can't be many miles from the ocean."

While they explored, the Indians had gone hunting for much needed food. When they came back to camp, the mark of fear was strong on the Indians' faces.

Perecute hurried to meet Captain Batts. "They heard the firing of a gun and the beating of drums while they were in the woods. The warring tribes are near!"

"We'll start back," Captain Batts said. "But first we will mark this spot and claim it for our king."

He and Fallam took branding irons with letters on them. They heated them to red hot in the fire and then each burned his initials on four trees. They also burned onto trees the name of Charles II, King of England, the name of the Virginia governor, and that of General Abraham Wood.

"One more mark," said Captain Batts. "We'll mark one tree with P for Perecute, who has been so faithful to us."

When that was done, the captain called out in a loud, clear voice, "We take this land for King Charles the Second. Long live King Charles, King of England, Scotland, Ireland and Virginia!"

He raised his rifle then, as did each man of the company. At a signal, they all fired together. Then, the ceremony over, the Indians and the three white men turned back the way they had come.

When they reached Fort Henry, they told General Wood of the river they had found. He, too, was excited over it. None of them knew that the high water mark was there because the weather had been dry and the river was "falling." Neither did they know that the "New River," as it came to be called, was really the upper end of the Kanawha River, which emptied into the Ohio River, not the ocean. The Ohio flows west to the Mississippi, which flows south to the Gulf of Mexico.

They did not know that beyond the second ridge of mountains were more mountains, ending with a ridge steeper than the others, and that finally beyond that was more wilderness, and many even greater mountains before the Pacific Ocean could be reached.

They told of the Great Warpath, not knowing as they did that it would be of more importance than the river they had found. In the days to come, the old Indian trail would be followed by almost every man who made his way over the Blue Ridge. His moccasins would join those of the Indians in wearing the Great Warpath wider and plainer. His horse's shoes would deepen it, too, and in time the Indian's trail would be the white man's road, leading from cabin to cabin and village to village. It was the first great trail to the Wilderness.

GABE ARTHUR WALKS THE WARRIORS' PATH

"This time, map the way to the Western Sea so that we can send traders there," General Wood told James Needham. It was a year and a half after Thomas Batts' trip over the Blue Ridge. Along with his work of getting more Indians to bring furs to Fort Henry, General Wood had been trying to get another exploring party to the land over the mountains. So far, all had been turned back by the roughness of the way or by unfriendly Indians.

"We'll do our best," James Needham said. He shook hands with General Wood and was ready to go.

General Wood reached up a hand to young Gabriel Arthur who sat on his horse waiting for the exploring party to start.

"Take care, Gabe, and good luck to you," said the general. Gabe had worked at Fort Henry since he had come to America from England. He was like a son to General Wood.

"I'll have stories to tell when we get back, General Wood," Gabe said as he shook hands. He fully expected to ride back into Fort Henry in about two months. It would be a year before he returned, and the stories he would tell would be of such adventures as no white boy had ever lived to tell.

Gabe found much to see as he rode with the others toward the mountains. To stay clear of an Indian village where another exploring party had been turned back, they swung farther to the south than Captain Batts had gone, into what is now North Carolina.

Some Cherokee Indians they met showed them the way to the Yadkin River valley. They headed west from there, and saw the Great Smoky Mountains with their crown of blue haze.

For four days they climbed up hills and rode down into valleys. Then they reached a ridge that was higher than the rest. James Needham noticed that from then on, the streams ran down the west side of the mountains instead of heading towards the Atlantic Ocean.

"Soon we should see the ocean of which Captain Batts spoke," Needham said, hopefully.

But they saw no ocean or great spreading valley

of mists. The going become rougher and rougher. Often they had to go through tangles of vines and briers. In the valleys they pushed through tall cane, sometimes eight or ten feet high. Its broken stalks were sharp and cut the horses' legs and feet. All the horses, but one sturdy animal, became too lame to go on.

Two weeks after they left the Yadkin Valley, they found a river which was larger than the others.

"Is this Captain Batts' river?" Needham wondered.

But the Cherokees told him, "Our river," and led the way to a log-walled village on its bank. The river that the Cherokees called theirs was the Tennessee.

The old chief came from the village to welcome them. Soon the explorers were inside, and welcoming feasts began.

Gabe was going to take the one horse they had left to a grassy place at the river bank where he could eat, drink and grow strong again. But the Cherokees had other ideas. They had seen the white man's horse before, but had never had a chance to be close to one for long.

"Tie him here," Gabe was told. The Indian pointed to a pole that stood in the middle of the village. Other Indians brought corn for the horse to eat and bear's oil with which to rub the cuts and sores on his legs and body. A circle of Indians almost always stood about watching him.

Nothing seemed to be too good for the visitors to the Cherokee village. They went to one feast after another, and watched dances in their honor by the hour. Needham found that the braves were more than willing to trade furs for some of the white man's things.

At the end of nine days, Needham called Gabe to one side.

"I shall go back to Fort Henry to tell General Wood what we have learned and bring back some trading goods. He will be disappointed that we haven't found a way to the sea, but I think he will be glad to know of the trade we can get.

"While I am gone, do all you can to learn their language, Gabe. Make friends, and tell them more about bringing furs to Fort Henry."

Gabe felt uneasy as he watched Needham leave. He was the only white man left in the village. But the Indians were willing to teach him their ways of working and playing. Soon he found the life pleasant, and the days passed quickly.

The old chief took a special interest in Gabe. He invited him to talk with him often, and let him sleep in his lodge.

By the end of June, Gabe began to look for Needham's return. When, one day, he heard a shouting outside the village, he thought it must be Needham and his guides.

"Or it could be the chief coming back from his hunt. He's been gone several days," the young man thought.

But there was a wild, angry note in the voices. There must be trouble of some sort. Gabe ran toward the opening in the log wall to learn what was happening.

"Where is Needham?" he asked, for he saw that these men were Needham's guides, but no white man was with them.

"Dead, as you soon will be!" a brave cried, and the returning Indians rushed forward. Gabe felt himself held by strong hands that dragged him toward the tall pole that stood in the village's center.

There, where only a few weeks ago they had shown such kindness to a lame horse, they tied him. They began a wild, screaming song and danced about the pole.

The Indians of the village were just as surprised as Gabe. At first they only listened and watched. But one after another joined in the mad dance. They stopped only to hear the words of the Indian who seemed to be the leader of the returning party.

"The white man has come to steal the Indian's hunting grounds!" he cried. "Kill him before he kills you! Kill every white man you see!"

Almost every man in the village joined the dancing and screaming. Drums were brought, and the singing and dancing took more form.

Gabe, not understanding why the Cherokees had turned against him, wished the end would come quickly. The wild voices and the pounding of the drums echoed in his head. The leather cords that bound him cut into his wrists and ankles. The Indians had ripped off his shirt, and his bare back already felt as if tongues of flame were licking it, the tongues of flame he knew would soon be a reality.

The women had begun to bring dry wood and

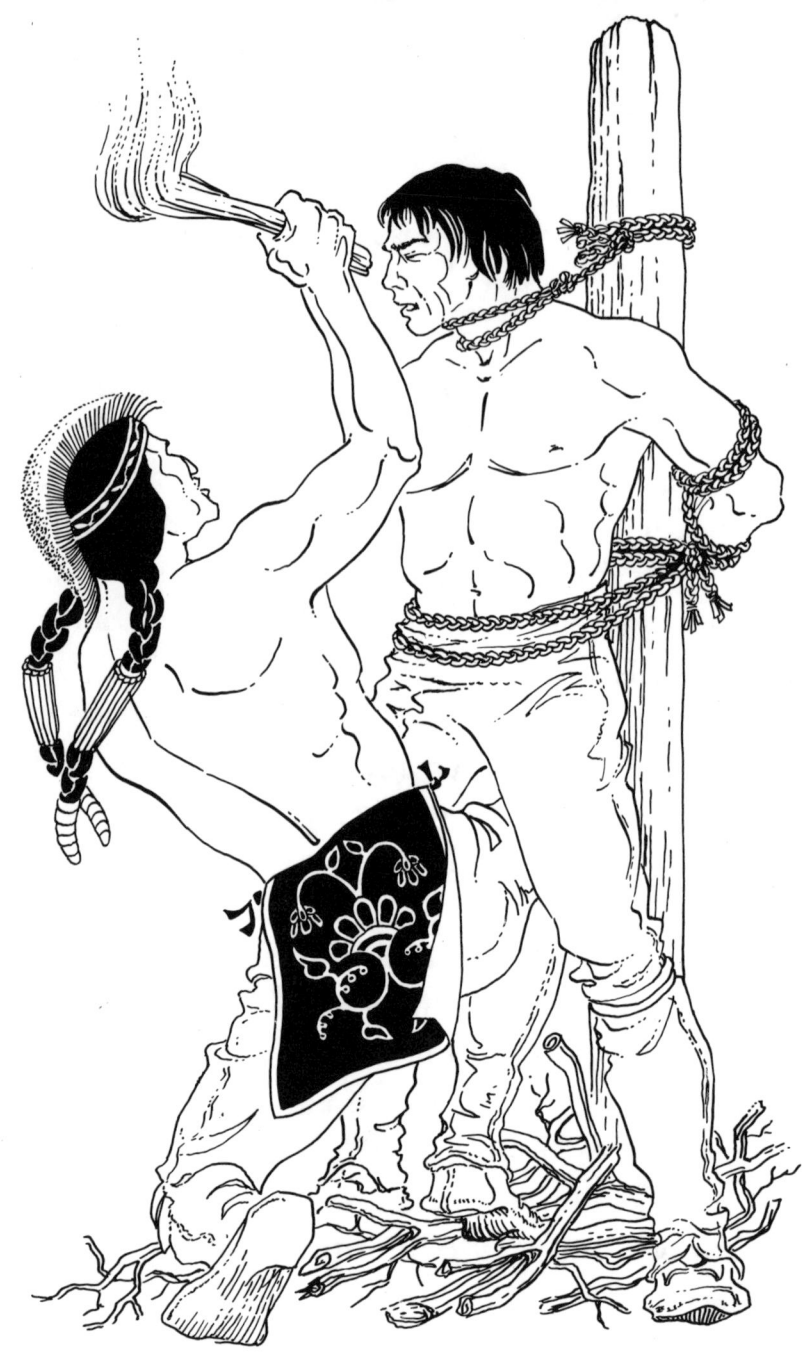

were piling it around him. Gabe knew that before long he would be only a pile of whitened bones. Sweat poured from every inch of his body. He closed his eyes against the sight of the crazed faces, but he could not shut out the wild sounds.

Then, as if cut by a tomahawk's blow, the sounds died. Gabe opened his eyes and saw the old chief. He stood outside the circle, his right hand upraised.

"Who takes the life of my friend?" he called out.

No one spoke. No one moved.

"Who is going to set fire to the good friend of his chief?" the old man cried then.

For a moment, stillness hung over the village. Then, as the bursting of a storm, the screaming began again. One man ran for burning torch.

"I kill this enemy of the Cherokee!" he cried, and ran towards the pile of dry sticks and cane. He bent down to light one side of the bonfire.

The chief's voice rang out in one word, "No!"

The brave did not rise until the flames began to lick through the pile. He stood up then and, as he did so, an arrow flew from the chief's bow. With one wild scream of pain, the brave fell.

The chief, helped by some of the braves who had

been with him on the hunt, hurried to cut the cords that held Gabe, and to pull him from the leaping flames.

There was no more dancing and singing that night. Gabe, sitting beside the chief in his lodge, heard the story one of Needham's guides told. He learned that Indian John, one of the guides from another tribe, had started the trouble. It was he who had killed Needham in their camp one morning. He had filled the other guides' heads with wild talk of what the white man meant to do until hatred for all white men sent them hurrying to the village to kill Gabe. Indian John himself had taken Needham's horse, gun and all his belongings and ridden away by himself.

The rest of that summer and all through the fall, Gabe was at the chief's side as the braves went to war and on to the fall hunt. He saw more of the land beyond the mountains than any white man had yet seen and lived to tell about it. He learned that the Tennessee River went a long way before it reached any ocean, and that Thomas Batts had been mistaken about New River, too.

Gabe began to look like an Indian, except for his hair, which was a sandy brown instead of black. Winter came, and he stayed on, almost like a member of the chief's family. He began to think he would never see a white man again. He knew that to start out in the wilderness by himself to find his way back to Fort Henry was to ask for death.

Late in the winter, something happened that made Gabe more sure than ever that he would not return to Fort Henry. His tribe went north to meet the Shawnees in battle. Somewhere in Kentucky the enemies met. Gabe, fighting from tree to tree, Indian style, felt an arrow hit his shoulder. As he fell to the ground, another went into his leg. When the Cherokees moved on, he could not follow fast enough and was captured.

He found himself half carried between silent Shawnee braves. They reached the Ohio River where they had canoes hidden near the bank. Gabe was pushed into one of them and taken across the river. From there the march went on to a village on the Scioto River, in what is now Ohio.

"This is the end of the trail for me," Gabe thought as he and the other prisoners were taken before the chief. He waited his turn for judgment, not showing the fear he felt. That much he had learned from the Cherokee. To show fear is to invite death.

His turn came. He stood before the Shawnee chief waiting for him to speak. But the chief only stared. Then he motioned to two of his braves and spoke a few words which Gabe could not hear. He found himself walking between the two men. They called to some women to follow, and all headed for the river.

Gabe found himself getting a scrubbing such as he had not had in a long time. The women had a bowl of wood ashes which they used in place of soap. They scrubbed at his skin as if to wash it off. The Indians chattered with excitement at its whiteness.

Back to the chief he went, dressed in fresh deerskin clothes. To his surprise, the chief handed him his gun, knife and metal hatchet. In sign language, the chief asked him to show what his tools and gun could do. Gabe showed him how easily his metal hatchet could chop wood, and how his knife could slice through leather. He had long ago run out of powder for his gun, so he could not show how it was used.

Again, Gabe found himself living the everyday life of an Indian. Again, the chief seemed pleased to have him near.

One day Gabe watched the Shawnee women getting a beaver ready to be cooked. The strong-tasting meat was not a favorite with the Indians, but good game was hard to find at the time. Gabe saw them hold the animal, fur and all, over the fire.

"They're burning off the hair! That's the part a trader would gladly pay for," he thought. An idea came into his head, an idea which could possibly win him his freedom.

He took another beaver, still with its fur on it, and hurried to the chief's lodge. Before the chief, he skinned the animal with his knife. He held up the fur, stroking it and looking at it to show how much it pleased him. Then he began to talk in sign language and the Cherokee tongue, trying to put across the idea that the white man in the east would give the Indians metal knives and hatchets like his own for the furs the Indians could get so easily. The

Indians could eat the meat, if they chose, and save the skin.

The chief seemed to understand. The next day, Gabe went to him again.

"Let me go to the white men's villages," he said. "I will send back traders with knives and hatchets."

The next day, Gabe was ready to leave. He was given a skin bag of dry corn meal to eat along the way.

"We will show you the way," the Shawnee braves told him. They took him across the Ohio River and then showed him the beginning of a path which led to the south. It was well worn and plain to see.

"The trail will take you to a place where you can go between the mountains," the Indians told Gabe. "Follow it across the grasslands, through the woods and over the hills. Good luck travels with you."

Day after day in that spring of 1674, almost one hundred years before the great pioneer Daniel Boone would use it to help him find his way through Kentucky, Gabriel Arthur walked the trail known as the *Warriors' Path*. He saw the salt licks where the deer and the buffalo and the smaller animals came, and the ashes of many Indian campfires. He crossed the pretty little streams which would someday furnish water for a settler's family. He walked through the deep, deep woods.

In all those days he saw no one. White men had not yet come to this wilderness; if Indian eyes watched him as he moved along the trail, southward and eastward, he did not know it. The trail took him into the roughness of the Cumberland Mountains, but never did it become too faint to follow.

At last he came to the place where the mountain wall opened. The trail led along the south side of the pass to a valley beyond. Gabe knew then that he was not far from the valley where his old tribe, the Cherokee lived and hunted. The trail swung south and took him to the village called Chota, where the Warriors' Path and the Great Warpath came together. The Cherokees gave him the help he needed to find his way back to Fort Henry.

He reached the fort after having been gone thirteen months.

General Wood could hardly believe his eyes when he saw that the "Indian" who came into the fort was really Gabe.

"I was sure you were dead, lad," the General said, and told Gabe the stories that had come back after Needham died.

Then it was Gabe's turn to tell of all that had happened to him. His stories widened the eyes of every man at the fort.

Gabe had never been to school, and could not write of Ohio and Kentucky and the trail that led to an opening in the mountain wall. But word passed from man to man, from father to son, and from then on it was told that there was a way through the mountains. The red men's secret was known.

THOMAS WALKER FOLLOWS A BUFFALO TRACE

Five men hacked their way through the thick brush and the tangling vines on the mountains of eastern Tennessee. Ahead of them, their hunting dogs yelped and barked, looking for the bears they were trained to find. The last man led a string of seven horses. The first five horses were saddled, but riding them was impossible on the rough mountain side. The last two carried the tools, food and camping supplies for a long journey.

Colby Chew, first man in the line, disappeared from the sight of the others for a moment. His voice brought good news back to the men who followed him.

"Dr. Walker, I've found a buffalo trail!"

Dr. Thomas Walker and the other three men caught up with Colby in a moment. They saw the worn path leading westward and mounted their horses again.

"We should soon come to the old Indian trace which leads to the Warrior's Path and the gap in the Cumberland Mountains," Dr. Walker told the others. "But we can't go much farther today. We'll make camp at that creek just ahead."

The men were in the same part of the country where Gabe Arthur had hunted with the Cherokee, and were looking for the trail Gabe had followed on his way back from captivity. But seventy-six years had gone by since Gabe's adventure. In those years a few white traders had followed the red men's trails into the land beyond the mountains. But none had tried to clear a patch of ground and build a cabin in the wilderness. No one had made a map of the red man's paths that led to the mountain pass.

In this spring of 1750, Dr. Walker and his men were on their way to look for good homelands over the last mountain ridge. Already the valley between the Blue Ridge and the next mountains was dotted with cabins and tiny settlements. Dr. Walker and his men had found one settler building his lonely cabin as far west as the Holston River valley. The Great Warpath that tied the new settlements together had become a wagon road. But since Dr. Walker's men had left that last cabin, they had traveled ten days in the wilderness.

As they moved along the buffalo trail, they could see the great wall of the Cumberland Mountains ahead. Dr. Walker knew that he must find the pass if they were to go much farther.

Just as the men were lifting the packs from the horses' backs, they heard the hunting dogs' barks turn into that excited sound that meant they had cornered a bear.

"Steaks for supper!" Dr. Walker cried. "Come on, Colby!" He reached for his rifle and climbed back into the saddle.

The dogs' baying became louder until it seemed to fill the woods. The two men rode until they could see the dogs. Just as they jumped from their horses, the voice of one dog turned into a cry of pain. Dr. Walker saw the dog fall to the ground and try to crawl away. A big bear stood on its hind legs, its back against a tree. The bear cuffed a dog who leaped for its throat. The dog fell back, but only to leap again.

Dr. Walker raised his rifle. He gave a sharp whistle and the dogs backed off. As the rifle boomed, the bear screamed and lunged. A second shot rang out from Colby's rifle, and the bear fell to the ground.

Dr. Walker ran forward, but his eyes were on the hurt dog and not on the bear. He kneeled beside the hound. A great long rip in the dog's side showed where the bear's claws had dug into him.

"Help me get this poor fellow up onto my horse, Colby," Dr. Walker said. "You can tend the bear afterwards."

A few minutes later, the doctor was back in camp with the dog. He sent another man to help Colby skin and butcher the bear. He himself took a leather case from one of the packs. It was the doctor's kit with which he had helped many people back in the days before he became a frontiersman. As tenderly as if the dog were a child, he bent to his work.

"You'll be all right, boy," he said to the whimpering dog. As if he understood, the dog looked at the doctor with trusting eyes.

The next morning, Dr. Walker's first thought was for the hurt dog. He seemed better, and when the men rode from their camp, Dr. Walker had the animal with him on his horse. There the dog rode each day until he was well enough to run.

Travel was slow for the next week. The buffalo trail led to the best river crossings, but the rivers were high from too much rain. Carrying their goods across was slow work. The horses ate too much of the green cane along the rivers and made themselves sick. The doctor would not go on until they were well again.

At each stop, one of the men, Ambrose Powell, pulled his sharp knife from its sheath and walked to a large beech tree.

"I'm going to make sure we can find our way back through this wilderness," he said. He dug his knife tip into the tree's silvery bark. When he had finished his work, his name marked the tree for as long as it stood. It told the men who came that way in later years that A. POWELL had been there before them. They found so many beech trees marked with his name that they named Powell River and Powell Mountain for him.

Each day the wall of the Cumberland Mountains seemed to grow higher and its sides steeper. Then suddenly at a creek crossing they found what they had been looking for.

"The Indian trail!" the leading man called back. It was easy to follow. In a short time, the men could see that its gentle climb was taking them to a break in the mountain wall. Before long they reached the pass itself. The trail followed along its south side.

"We'll camp here," Dr. Walker decided. He wanted to write his notes on how they had found the pass and mark it on his map so that it could be found again and again. In his mind's eye, he saw hundreds of people moving through this pass to homes in the great western wilderness.

The men went exploring. Colby Chew heard the sound of rushing water on the north side of the pass.

"Come see this spring!" he called to Dr. Walker.

The doctor hurried to see what Colby had found. "I do believe it has enough water to turn a mill wheel," he said. "Don't you, Colby?"

But Colby was pulling himself up the rock wall above the falling water. He called out, as he pulled some bushes aside, "Cold air coming out of this hole, Doctor! There must be a big cave back in there. I'm going in to see."

Colby disappeared. A few minutes later, he crawled back out again. "Too dark to see much," he said. "But there is a river flowing in the cave. Likely this spring comes from that underground river."

"We'll call this passage *Cave Gap*," Dr. Walker decided, and marked it clearly on his map. Then the men went on, following the Warrior's Path to the land beyond the mountains.

A few days later, they found the river Dr. Walker named the *Cumberland* after an English duke. To cross it, the men had to make a bark canoe, using the bark of an elm tree. Then, in the Cumberland Valley, in what is now southeastern Kentucky, Dr. Walker found the first good farming land he had seen so far. There wasn't much, but a nice stretch of flat land lay along the river.

"Well, boys," he said, "This is better land. We'll build a cabin here." He walked to the spot which seemed best to him.

Ambrose Powell said, "Why build a cabin, Doctor? We aren't any of us set to stay here."

Dr. Walker was again seeing those hundreds of people to come. "No, Ambrose. But it will show our claim to the land. And it will be a welcome shelter to the settlers as they come by. I would like three of you to stay here to build it while I go on to find more land."

The men drew lots to see who was to go on with

Dr. Walker. Then the three who stayed began to work. A new sound rang out in the Kentucky woods, the sound of axes against tree trunks. In three days, the men had a cabin built. It was twelve feet wide and eighteen feet long.

When it was finished, Dr. Walker had not come back.

"He said to plant some corn next," one of the men said. "Dr. Walker thinks he may be bringing some people back here later this summer, and it would be a fine thing to have a field of corn ready for harvest."

The three men scratched in the rich river bottom land and dropped in some of the corn seeds Dr. Walker had brought on the journey. They found some peach stones in the pack, too, and they planted them in the hope a peach orchard would grow there.

Dr. Walker still had not returned.

"Let's take a day to go hunting for bear," the men decided.

The hunt was a good one, but if they were to keep the meat, it would have to be packed in salt.

"Remember the salt lick we saw a few miles back?

We can leave a note here for Dr. Walker and go there to make salt," said Ambrose.

They packed their camp kettles onto the horses and set off for the spring where salty water came from the ground. By boiling the water away, they "made" salt.

They were gone from the new cabin for several days. It stood lonely and silent when they returned. But the next day, there was a call from the edge of the clearing, and the two who had been exploring rode up to the cabin door.

Dr. Walker again had a hurt dog riding with him. He passed the dog down to Ambrose before he dismounted.

"What did you find? How far does the good land reach?" the men asked.

Dr. Walker did not answer at first. He chose to look over the cabin and see the work the three men had done before telling his story.

"You did well," he said, but he looked unhappy. Then he looked back toward the mountains beyond the stretch of river bottom.

"I was to find thousands of acres of land to be sold to settlers," he said sadly. "What did I find?

This one little stretch of river bottom, and mile after mile after mile of mountains like those you see around you. The land is so rough and full of stones that a man would break his back trying to farm it."

He went to his pack and took out his doctor's kit. "I'll need some of that bear grease, Ambrose," he said, and went to work caring for a lame horse and for one that had been bitten on the nose by a snake.

"As soon as the horses are well, we shall start back," he said. But the lame horse did not improve, no matter how the doctor tried to help him.

"I don't like to do it, but we shall have to leave him here," Dr. Walker said. "He is old, and the journey was too much to ask of him."

Just before a bend in the trail cut off their view, Dr. Walker and the other men stopped for a last backward look. The first young shoots of corn were up in the little field. The old white horse was grazing near the cabin door. Again the dream of settlement brightened Dr. Walker's eyes. He called out, as he turned his horse into the trail, "We'll be back!"

Before heading homeward, he tried again to find good farmland. But this time as before, he circled about, staying in the mountains, not knowing that a little to the west the hills became gentle. But his journey was not wasted, for from that time on, the pass through the forbidding mountain wall was on the maps. Dr. Walker's *Cave Gap* became *Cumberland Gap,* and his dream of hundreds of settlers going through it was to come true.

The little cabin the men built was the first house in what would become the state of Kentucky. Its cornfield and its peach trees fed only the wandering hunters and traders who passed that way. In time, the cabin in the woods rotted away.

But it was not forgotten. Many years later, axes rang out again in that woods as men built another cabin just like it to stand in its place. There, in Dr. Thomas Walker State Park, it stands today.

WASHINGTON AND THE FRENCH INDIAN

"Hello, there! Are you Mr. Gist?"

Christopher Gist stopped his work of loading dried ears of corn into a wagon. He was getting ready to move from his log cabin home in the Yadkin River valley to a new cabin he had built on the trail to the Ohio country. He saw two men riding toward him, with a string of pack horses behind them.

"I am Christopher Gist," he called in answer and walked toward the strangers.

His visitors were not frontiersmen like himself. They wore the clothes of Tidewater gentlemen. It was not often that such men made their way as far west as the little settlements of the Yadkin Valley.

The men got down from their horses and Christopher saw that the leader was tall, slim, and much younger than he had first thought. "About twenty-one." Christopher decided.

The young man held out his hand and said, "I

am Major George Washington, and this is Lieutenant Van Braam, Mr. Gist. We have ridden here with a message from the governor of Virginia at Williamsburg."

Major Washington took a folded paper from his saddlebag. He said, "Perhaps you had better read the governor's letter, Mr. Gist, to understand why we are here and why we wish to have you travel with us."

"Travel with you? But, gentlemen, I am just about to leave on a trip with my family. We are moving to a fine new place I found on my trip to the Ohio country three years ago in 1750."

But Christopher unfolded the paper and began to read.

As he finished, Major Washington spoke eagerly. "You see, Mr. Gist, because you made that exploring trip to the Ohio country three years ago, you are the only man who can guide us now. You know the trail, you know how to live in the wilderness, the Indians think of you as a friend, and our government trusts you."

Christopher turned towards the cabin. "Come inside, gentlemen. We'll talk it over."

Christopher Gist was an unusual frontiersman. He had been to school in the years before he became a pioneer and could write good reports and read with understanding. He had been trained for the work of a surveyor, and could measure and map the wild land. He knew when to talk, and when to be quiet. For those reasons, he had been sent into the western wilderness in the fall of the same year that Dr. Walker had gone through Cumberland Gap. He, too, had gone to find land for settlement.

But Christopher Gist had been sent farther north. He had been asked to look for good farm land along the Ohio River and north of the river toward Lake Erie. In the "Ohio Country" he traveled with some traders and visited Indian villages as far west as the Miami Valley in western Ohio. He found miles of good farming country.

He thought about that long journey as he listened to the talk around the dinner table. Mrs. Gist had quickly added two more wooden plates to those laid out for the family. The two men from the east seemed to enjoy the simple meal of squirrel stew and corn bread. Christopher learned that Lt. Van Braam had served in the Dutch army before he

came to America to be a teacher. Major Washington had brought him along because he could speak French.

"You see, Mr. Gist," George Washington explained, "we are to journey all the way to the French forts near Lake Erie. Lt. Van Braam will help me in my talks with the French leaders. We must make it clear to them that the Ohio country belongs to the English, and that the French must leave."

Christopher said, "The French say the Ohio River Valley is theirs! When I was in Ohio three years ago, they were trying to make the Indians trade with them and not with our traders. They went so far as to make prisoners of some of our traders."

"You understand why it is important for you to go with us then, Mr. Gist," Washington said. "You will go, won't you?"

Gist thought the matter over once more. It was clear that these Tidewater men needed a guide. He knew of no one else who could go in his place. His family would have to wait a few weeks to move to the new settlement.

"Yes, I will go as your guide," he said. "Now let

us plan what we will need for so long a journey. It is already the middle of November, and we shall be traveling in the worst of the winter weather."

And so, with four frontiersmen from a trading post near Gist's home, they set out. They journeyed north over the Great Warpath almost to the Potomac River. There they cut west, following a lesser Indian trail, crossed the Potomac at the trading post of eighty-three-year-old Thomas Cresap, and swung north and west again.

Colonel Cresap had been working on the trail beyond his post, making it into a narrow road. But even so, the going was slow as they crossed a mountain ridge. In a valley once more, they headed north, past Christopher's new settlement, where the first cabins were standing ready for his family.

John Frazier's post was their last stop where there was a roof over their heads and a friendly fire. Frazier helped them cross the Allegheny River by sending his men in a big canoe to carry the packs to the land west of the Allegheny and north of the Ohio. They swam their horses across.

Northward they went, through mile after mile of Indian country, until they reached the first of the

French forts. Major Washington delivered his message, only to be told that the French did not plan to leave the Ohio country. After he had visited Fort LeBoeuf, just a little south of Lake Erie, Washington was ready to go south again.

"And the faster, the better," he told Christopher. "I must get back to Williamsburg to tell the governor that we must bring an army up here and build some strong forts. If we don't act quickly, we will lose this land forever."

But it was almost Christmas Day when they could start. Winter had set in. The creeks were freezing over so that the ice had to be broken to give the horses and the men water to drink. The grass along the trail was too poor to feed the horses well, and they were growing weak.

On Christmas Day, Washington decided that they were traveling much too slowly. He called Christopher Gist to his side.

"Christopher, we must get word to the governor faster than these horses can make the journey. Now, here is my plan. You and I will set out on foot and take a short cut down to Frazier's trading post. There we can get fresh horses to finish the trip."

Christopher stared at Major Washington, hardly believing his ears. This young man talked as if walking one hundred fifty miles on snow and ice through Indian country was the same as riding to town on a summer's day!

"But, Major!" he gasped. "Do you have any idea how far it is, and how cold it can be sleeping out in the open in winter?"

"Certainly," said Major Washington.

"And if we meet unfriendly Indians? You know the French leaders are paying the northern tribes to attack us."

"We are two strong men, able to take care of ourselves."

"But," sputtered Christopher, "you have never *walked* a whole day in your life! It would be too hard on you."

Washington drew himself up tall. "Mr. Gist," he said, "are you afraid to take this journey with me?"

"Certainly not. I am thinking only of your safety."

"Then it is settled," said Washington. "I shall change to clothing like yours and prepare a pack. Lt. Van Braam will be in charge of the horses. Be ready for an early start."

Christopher tried once more. "To leave the trail in the wilderness is risky at the best of times. In winter and through Indian country it could cost your life."

"I will take the risk, Mr. Gist. As for finding our way, you and I are both trained surveyors. We have our compasses, and you are an expert woodsman. We can do it."

Christopher gave up. He could not help but admire the way the young major put the good of his country ahead of his own safety. George Washington was the kind of young man the colonies needed.

The morning of December 26 was very cold. The two men started out, each with a pack on his back and a rifle in his hand. Christopher led the way at a fast clip. A man had to move fast to keep his feet from freezing. For the start of the journey, they followed the trail to the south, but at an Indian village a few miles ahead, they would leave the trail and head east toward the Allegheny River.

By afternoon, the wind had turned even colder. "The deep rivers will freeze solid if this keeps up,"

Christopher said. "That will help us. We can cross on the ice."

Washington did not talk much as they went on. In the middle of the afternoon, Christopher saw the set lines on the young major's face.

"There's an old cabin ahead," Christopher said. "An eighteen mile walk is enough for our first day on foot. We'll stop there for the night."

Washington smiled then. "Fine," he said. "But we'll make an early start tomorrow."

Washington could hardly keep his eyes open after Christopher had a fire going in the little empty cabin. They had strips of dried meat and corn meal in their packs, and from these they made a meal, Indian style. Then they rolled up in their blankets on the dirt floor. Sleep came quickly.

At two in the morning, Christopher heard the major say, "Mr. Gist, wake up. We had better get started."

As they left the hut a little later, Christopher was glad there was snow on the ground. Without it, he could have lost his way, especially after the trail entered a deep woods. The major followed close behind him, even when he walked fast.

"I didn't think you'd be so spry this morning, Major," Christopher said. "That was a long walk yesterday for a man who has never traveled on foot."

George Washington's every muscle ached, but he said, "I'll keep up with you, Christopher."

By noon, they reached the Indian village where they planned to leave the trail. While they were resting and eating, an Indian came and sat down beside them.

"Howdy, Annosanah," the Indian said to Christopher.

Annosanah was the name the Indians had given Christopher when he stayed in their villages three years before. It meant "good man." He was startled to hear it now. Where had he seen this Indian before? Was it back in one of the French forts?

"Where you go, Brother Annosanah?" the Indian asked.

"We are returning to Virginia," Gist said.

The Indian looked around questioningly. "Where are your horses?"

Major Washington spoke then. "We are traveling on foot because we are in a hurry. Perhaps you know this country well. Could you take us to the

Allegheny River by the shortest way?"

Christopher thought he saw a strange look on the Indian's face, as though he had some sudden, secret joy. He wished the major had not spoken as freely.

When the Indian spoke, his eyes told nothing. He said, "Yes, white brothers. I can lead you. Wait here."

He hurried off to one of the lodges. About ten minutes later he was back, rifle in hand and a small pack on his back. He reached for Washington's pack and put it on his back, too.

"Carry rifle, too," he said.

But Major Washington said, "No, thank you. I'll carry my rifle."

The three set out, the Indian walking ahead quite fast. One mile, two miles, three miles they went on eastward through the woods. George Washington began to lag behind.

"I'll have to ask him to slow down," he said.

The Indian turned about and said, "I will carry the Major's gun for him." He reached out to take it, but George Washington held onto it.

"No, thank you. I'll carry it myself. Just slow down a bit."

On they went, not quite so fast as before. After another two miles, George was limping badly.

"Guide," he said. "We will have to make camp at the next place where there is water."

The Indian stopped. Then he turned around to face Gist and Washington, but before he spoke he looked fearfully about him. "Oh, no, must not camp near here. There are enemy Indians in these woods! We must go farther."

"We'll take the risk," Washington said.

The Indian grunted and turned about. As he walked on, Gist stood still a moment to read his compass. As he had guessed, they were swinging more to the north than to the south. He said nothing, not wanting to alarm Washington. But this fellow would bear watching.

They came to a creek. "We can camp here," Washington said.

The Indian said, "Not good. Enemy scalp you as you sleep."

"We'll stand watch in turn," Gist said.

The Indian was silent a moment. Then, in a pleasant voice, he said, "My cabin not far, and we be safe there."

Major Washington liked the idea of a dry floor under him as he slept, even the dirt floor of an Indian cabin. He said, "Let me rest my feet a little, and then we shall go to your cabin."

In a little while, he was ready to try again. When they had gone another mile, he asked, "Where is your cabin? We are traveling too far north. If your cabin is far out of our way, it will be better if we do not go there."

Christopher was not too surprised to learn that the Major had also noticed that they were going northward. He was glad that Washington, too, would now be on guard.

The Indian said, "The cabin is just as far as a gun could be heard. Not far at all."

Saying nothing, Washington and Gist followed him for another mile.

"Guide," Washington said then, "we have traveled as far as a gun could be heard or farther. Where is your cabin?"

The Indian turned with a smile, "It is close now. Just two whoops away."

"How are your feet now, Major?" Christopher asked.

Washington's mouth twisted. "I can scarcely feel them now, Christopher. We may as well follow a little farther and have a roof over our heads tonight."

The Indian led on another two miles. Ahead was an open meadow, sloping gently away from them. It was very likely that an ice-covered stream would be at the foot of the slope.

Major Washington called to the Indian to stop.

"Guide," he said, "your idea of distance is not mine. We shall camp here."

They walked out of the woods into the open meadow. As Gist and Washington headed down toward the frozen stream, the Indian swung off to the left. Suddenly there was a loud bang. Gist and Washington dropped quickly to the ground.

"Are you shot?" Major Washington called to Gist.

"No," said Christopher. He saw the Indian run to a large white oak tree which stood in the meadow. "I'll kill him for that!" he said, and started forward.

George Washington was beside Christopher as he reached the Indian who, behind the tree, was busily reloading his gun. Christopher had pulled his hatchet from his belt and was raising it over the Indian's head when Washington grabbed his arm.

"No, Christopher. Let's see what he has to say for himself." Then he turned to the Indian. "I suppose you were lost and fired your gun," he said.

The Indian saw that his scalp was safe. Coolly, he said, "Oh, no, Major. I know the way. I just fired my gun to tell my squaw to get meat cooking for us."

"We'll do without meat," the Major said. "Now get a campfire made for us."

The three walked to the little stream's bank. The major and Christopher stayed close to the Indian, giving him no chance to use his loaded gun. They put down their packs and the Indian began to gather firewood.

"Dry wood back in woods," he said.

"We'll take care of your rifle so you'll have both hands free to gather wood," Major Washington said. The Indian could think of no reason to keep his rifle with him. He went to the woods without it.

"I don't trust that fellow," Washington said. "I believe he is just waiting for the moment when he can kill us both."

"Then your message will never get to Virginia," Gist said. "Why don't we kill him first?"

But Washington shook his head. "No. If we do, a

war party will kill the next white men they find to get even. We must get rid of him in another way."

The Indian was returning.

"Where is your cabin from here?" Gist asked.

The Indian dropped the firewood. He smiled, an eager look on his face. "Just a little way over the hill. Why don't we go there? Have meat to eat."

"The major can't walk any farther today," Gist said. "We'll make our camp here. But you may go to your cabin if you wish. We will follow your track in the morning."

The Indian looked sharply at Gist and then at Washington. Their faces told him nothing.

"You need my help to find the Allegheny," he said.

George Washington was brushing snow aside, fixing a place to unroll his blanket. "My feet will be better in the morning," he said. "We will be glad to have you guide us to the river. Go to your squaw, if you wish."

Gist had another idea which would make the Indian sure that he and Washington meant to camp at this spot for the night. He looked into his pack and pulled out some hard, dry biscuits.

"Here is a cake of bread for you," he said. "You

take it, and when we come to your cabin in the morning, you must give us meat."

The Indian seemed satisfied. He took his rifle, his pack, and the dry bread and set off. When he was out of sight, Gist climbed the little rise of ground. From the top, he could see the Indian walking on towards the woods. He felt sure the fellow would not be back for at least an hour.

He hurried back to the camp. "Now, Major, we will be on our way and go as far as we can before darkness comes."

Major Washington said nothing, but rolled up his blanket and put his pack together again. The two men were soon on their way in the opposite direction from that the Indian had taken. After they had gone about a half mile, they stopped to rest and eat, but only for a short time.

"Can you travel again, Major?" Gist asked. "The more distance we put between ourselves and that Indian before daylight comes, the better."

"I'm ready, Christopher," Washington said. As he stood, his tightened lips were the only sign of the pain and weariness he felt. "Lead the way."

All through the night they walked. In the morning, they rested an hour, and then went on. Not until night came again did they feel safe enough to sleep. The "French Indian" was seen no more.

WASHINGTON AND THE WILD ALLEGHENY

Christopher Gist and Major George Washington slept so soundly after their long walk to escape the French Indian that neither of them felt the night air grow colder. But with the first gray light, Christopher opened his eyes.

He shivered. But instead of rolling his blanket tighter about him, he sat up, rubbed his hands and face to warm them up a bit, and then got up to rebuild the fire.

"Major, wake up, before you freeze to death," he said. He touched Washington's shoulder. George opened his eyes.

"I see we're both still here," he said. "That Indian must have decided we weren't worth following. Perhaps he froze in his tracks. It's cold enough!"

He stood up and moved about, trying out his sore feet and aching muscles.

"Can you walk a few miles today?" Christopher asked. "The Allegheny River can't be much farther. From there it is less than a day's march to Frazier's.

It is even possible that we can sleep by a warm fire tonight, Major."

"That sounds like heaven, Christopher. This nippy air and the thought of a warm room will keep me moving along, no matter how my feet and muscles ache."

Christopher had chopped a hole in the ice of the creek near their camp to get water for making coffee. It was hot and strong, and after drinking it both men felt better. They packed up their goods and started out over the frozen ground.

They had gone only three miles or so when they came to the edge of the woods. Below, at the foot of a steep bank, was a river. The men could hear the sound of rushing water.

Christopher said, "The Allegheny. I'd know it from most other rivers in these parts anytime. It runs along as if it couldn't get where it's going fast enough."

George looked down at the black band of water that ran between iced-over edges of the river. As he watched, a mass of ice chunks came tossing along, as though hurrying toward the peaceful Ohio for needed rest.

"It is beautiful, Christopher, but how are we going to cross it? That ice along the shore reaches out only about fifteen feet," Washington said.

Christopher led the way down the bank. "I thought it would be frozen over, but the Allegheny doesn't give up easily. The only thing we can do is to build ourselves a raft."

They began the work of cutting young trees with the one tool they had, Christopher's hatchet. By noon, the raft was hardly begun. The work took all afternoon, and the sun was about to drop below the western hills when at last they pushed the raft to the ice at the river's edge.

"Well, Christopher," said George, "we can make it over the river before dark. Even if we can't get to Frazier's tonight, I'll feel better and sleep easier, knowing that Indian and his friends won't cross the Allegheny to scalp us in our sleep."

But Christopher had gone back to the grove of young trees. "We'll each need a pole, Major. The raft will be hard to guide to the ice on the other side. We'll be fighting the current every inch of the way."

Washington shivered as he waited for Christopher

to cut the poles. The sun had shone all day, but there was little heat in it. The wind whipped down the river valley, sharp and cold.

Christopher brought the poles. "It is so cold that I don't see how that river keeps running," he said.

"There are more and more ice chunks coming with it," George said. "I wouldn't care to try to swim it today."

Both men strapped their packs to their backs. They tied their rifles on the packs to leave both hands free for poling the raft.

"Let's hope we won't have to swim, Major," Christopher said. "Are you all set? Then let's push off."

The two pushed their clumsy little raft to the edge of the ice. As the water took hold of it, they jumped aboard.

"Work fast, or we'll go all the way to the Monongahela," Christopher said.

Both men pushed with their poles to try to head the raft across the water. The raft creaked, and water pushed up between the logs.

"The raft won't hold together long enough to take us anywhere near the Monongahela," Washington said between pushes with his pole. "It could pull apart any minute."

The river was carrying them downstream fast. But they had inched their way almost to the middle when Christopher saw a great mass of ice chunks heading for the raft.

"Look out! Ice!" he cried.

Both men pushed hard to try to get the raft clear of the ice. But it was no use. The ice hit the raft. It closed in around the logs, trying to lock the raft into itself to carry it wildly down the river.

Washington gave a great shove at the ice to try to push it clear. It pulled away with a sudden crashing sound. George found himself being carried with it, pole and all.

"Let go of the pole!" Christopher shouted. But George did not need to be told. His pole rode down the river, like a toothpick stuck into the ice mass. But in the surprise of the moment, he was thrown into the river.

A wave washed over the raft and almost took Christopher with it. He threw himself face down, reaching back towards Washington with outstretched arms.

"Swim with the current, Major!" he cried. "I can help you onto the raft!"

With all his strength, George Washington swam to catch up with the raft. After a minute which seemed more like ten, Christopher was helping him from his ice bath, letting the raft go where it would.

"Major, you'll freeze to death, unless we can get to shore and build a fire right away," Christopher said, worry showing on his face and in his voice.

Washington's teeth were chattering so that he could hardly speak, but he raised his arm and pointed down the river.

"B-b-brace yourself!" he cried.

Christopher turned quickly. The raft was heading straight for an island. It hit the ice at the island's edge with a crashing of wood and ice. Both men jumped for the shore. The pieces of the raft caught in the floating ice, and down the river they went.

"There goes a good day's work," said Christopher. "But this island is a blessing, Major. We are on land, and I can build a fire to dry out your clothing."

He undid his pack as soon as he had found enough twigs, leaves and bits of bark to start a fire. He took his dry blanket and gave it to Washington to use until his own could be dried. Then off he went for more wood, and soon the fire was blazing high. With forked branches, Christopher built drying racks, and soon Washington's clothing and blanket were steaming in the warmth.

Christopher went on working. He brought a few poles and boughs of evergreen to build a little shelter near the fire, to break the wind. Before he had finished, he knew that he had frozen his finger tips on his right hand. But his mind was on the wellbeing of the major. He brought water in a kettle and put it over the fire. Hot coffee would help warm him up.

A little later, Washington said, "My teeth have stopped chattering, thanks to you, my friend. Without you, I'd be a dead man now." His eyes met Gist's in a look that showed each liked and admired the other.

"We'll stay close to the fire and keep it going all night, Major, or both of us may yet be dead," Christopher said. "Even so, we must move about often to keep our blood moving. It must be below zero right now."

"And to think we dreamed of spending tonight at John Frazier's!" said Washington. "In the morning, we'll face this wild Allegheny River with better luck, I hope."

Luck was with them, too, for in the morning they found a silvery stretch of ice from the island to the shore, solid enough to carry them across. They went on the ten miles to John Frazier's trading post. That night their sleep was sound.

As they traveled the rest of the homeward trail, now on fresh horses, George Washington and Christopher Gist talked of the bad news they brought from the Ohio country, and of the struggle between the French and the English-Americans.

"We must get forts built if we are to hold the Ohio country," Washington said. "The point of land where the Allegheny and the Monongahela Rivers come together is a perfect place. It is the *gateway to the Ohio*."

Washington and Gist were right. Trouble came between the French and the English-Americans. Soon after their journey to the Ohio country, a war began. It was called the *French and Indian War,* and while it lasted no one could build homes in the Ohio country, or in Kentucky.

As soon as Washington delivered his message, the governor of Virginia sent men to begin a fort at the "gateway to the Ohio," where Pittsburgh stands now. But the French and their Indians attacked it before it was finished and drove the Virginians away. The French built a large, strong fort on the point.

The trail to the Ohio country, where old Thomas Cresap worked to build a road, became a roadway for the soldiers who went north to try to win back the important fort where the Ohio River begins. It was called Braddock's Road then, named for the general who led the men to battle, only to be beaten by few French soldiers and their Indians, fighting Indian style.

Major Washington had become Colonel Washington and was on the trail he and Gist had traveled as one of Braddock's officers. He built a fort, called Fort Necessity, a few miles south of Gist's new settlement on the trail. As for Gist, he, too, was busy with the war. He and his oldest son were scouts for General Braddock. Dr. Thomas Walker was there, too, in charge of supplies.

Men widened the trail and made log bridges so that the supplies could be carried to the soldiers in wagons. The wagons creaked up and down the road, driven by men who chose that as their way of helping win the war.

At night, the wagoners made camp together whenever they could. After their supper was eaten, they sat for a while around a cheerful campfire. The shadows in the woods reminded them of other nights in the many wilderness woods they had seen. They told stories of their adventures, sometimes true but often embroidered to make the storytellers into heroes.

One of the storytellers was a man named John Finley. He had been in the Ohio country and in Kentucky, too, trading with the Indians. He saw the light in the blue eyes of one of his listeners, a young fellow from the frontier hills whose name was Daniel Boone. John's stories grew better, and the land over the mountains became a paradise on earth as he talked of it.

Dreams were born in young Daniel Boone's heart those evenings on the trail, dreams that would never die. They were dreams of following the trails to the wilderness, to the land where a man could be free.

PEDDLER WITH A PACK OF DREAMS

The years went by, and at last the French and Indian Wars were over. France lost, and gave up her claims to the Ohio Valley. But still no white settlement grew in that land beyond the mountains. Dr. Walker's cabin had stood, empty and lonely, for almost twenty years.

On a spring day in 1769, a peddler made his slow way down the Yadkin Valley road in North Carolina, going from cabin to cabin to sell his wares. He drew near a certain cabin where a black-haired woman and four little girls heard the clanging and the banging of the pots and pans he had for sale. They hurried to the doorway to watch his coming, not knowing that with him came a pack of dreams, dreams which would change their lives and the lives of hundreds of other people. They were dreams that would open the trails to the wilderness.

The peddler called out, "Whoa!" He climbed down from his tired old saddle horse. The clanging and the banging stopped as the pack horse which followed stopped and sagged into stillness. On its back, long-handled spoons and chimney cranes stuck out like porcupine quills. Above the packs a wooden frame was set, and from it hung iron and copper kettles and pans. Both horses closed their eyes as their heads dropped forward. Their master would go inside the cabin to bring to the lady the bits of news he had gathered on the way in exchange for a cup of coffee and a sample of the lady's best baking.

"Howdy, Ma'am!" the peddler called out cheerfully to the woman in the doorway. A baby girl was in her arms. Another, about three years old, pulled at her mother's long brown skirt and half hid behind her. Two more girls, five and seven years old, had been pounding kernels of dry corn into meal in a hollowed stump near the cabin. They stopped their work and stood staring at the peddler.

"Winter's about over, Ma'am. The sunshine's nice and warm today." The peddler took a battered beaver hat from his head and wiped his brow with a red handkerchief.

The woman nodded. "Likely so. My man's getting the field ready for planting now." She looked off in the direction of the small clearing beyond the

house. Two boys and a slender man in brown buckskins were crossing the clearing, coming to see who the caller was. The peddler guessed the boys to be just a year or so apart in age, perhaps ten and eleven years old.

"Here he comes now, along with James and Israel," the woman said. "Won't you come in and have coffee with us? Or maybe you can stay for supper . . ."

But she saw the man was not listening. He had been staring at the man coming from the field. Now he walked toward him a few steps.

"Dan'l! Could you be Daniel Boone, the same that was on the wagon road with Braddock?"

The frontiersman was grinning widely, "Well, I'll be jiggered," he said. "I'd know that voice anywhere . . . used to put me to sleep nights on Braddock's Road. John Finley, you old horse-trader, what are you doing here?"

Mrs. Boone spoke up. "He came to sell me some new pots and pans, Dan'l, but so far we hadn't got past the weather."

Pots and pans seemed far from John Finley's mind as he and Daniel Boone talked over the days, fourteen years ago, when the two of them had been wagoners.

James and Israel led the old horses to the stable yard behind the cabin, took off saddles and packs, and gave them hay and water. Susannah and Jemimah, the two older girls, set the rough board table with an extra place.

"Ye'll stay the night with us, of course," Daniel said, and John Finley agreed.

After supper, while Mrs. Boone and the girls cleared up, the two men settled down before the fireplace.

"What have you been doing these fourteen years, besides raising young'uns?" Finley asked. "I can see why you married Rebecca, here, the more so after eating some of her cooking. But I remember you as a young fellow who wanted to see more of the world than his own clearing. You wanted to travel to far places."

"And I did, some," Daniel said. He rested his feet on a section of log and leaned his hickory chair back onto two legs. "I've been to Florida. Thought maybe it would be a good place to live, now that the Yadkin Valley is gettin' to be so crowded. A man needs plenty of elbow room, and ye scarce can find it here anymore."

Daniel got up and poked at the fire. Then he went on, teetering back in his chair as he talked. "Rebecca didn't want to go to Florida, so I let my claim there go. Too wet for good hunting, anyway. And you know, John, I count on hunting to make a living for me and my family. Got to go where there are good deerskins and beaver furs to get money to buy pots and pans from the likes of you. Can't scratch much out of this farm land."

Rebecca spoke up then. "Dan'l, you know you could 'scratch' more out of it if you could stay with it long enough. But you're always going off with your rifle, as soon as the seeds are in the ground. The poor plants have to do with what care the children and I can give them." Her voice was scolding, but she looked at Daniel and smiled as she finished speaking. The smile said she'd not trade her restless hunter for a settled farmer.

Daniel said, "You know I promised you I'd always come back. When I went to Florida, I said I'd be home for Christmas. And when did I get back?"

"On Christmas Day," Rebecca said, and laughed.

Daniel stood again and took a long rifle from the wooden pegs which held it above the mantel. He set to work cleaning it as he went on talking. "Old *Tick-Licker* here and I have gone on many a hunting trip. We've been west beyond the Holston Valley. James has been with me, too, all through these hills. He and I stayed out in the woods three months last year. Had a pretty good hunt, too."

Finley's eyes lighted up. He said, "Dan'l, now I can see the fellow I used to know. You've still got those itchy feet. I remember you as the fellow with the greatest longing to see the land on the other side of the mountains of anyone I ever knew. I believe you've still got the wish to go see that great land of Kentucky."

Rebecca spoke sharply. "Don't you be putting notions into Dan'l's head. Yadkin country is where he belongs."

"Now, Rebecca," said Daniel, "I'm not so sure about that. Taxes are getting high, and the governor wants money for this and that—money we don't have. A man's got to go into good hunting land to get skins and furs just to pay so's he can keep his home." He held *Tick-Licker* up and looked the length of the long barrel. Then he spoke again, with a new note of interest in his voice. "Tell me more about Kentucky, John."

John talked on and on, long after all the children but James had curled up on the bumpy, corn-shuck mattresses for the night. Rebecca fell asleep in her chair, but Daniel and eleven-year-old James listened wide-eyed to tales of the wonderful hunting on the other side of the mountain wall, in the land of the waving blue grass.

John told how he had gone down the Ohio River as a trader just two years before. He landed on the Kentucky shore, and found the Indians friendly and ready to trade. He built a little trading post in the middle of Kentucky, and the Indians brought in the furs they took so easily. Back up the Ohio he went with all the furs he could load into a large canoe.

"A dollar a piece for deerskins, Dan'l. It's easy money. I've been wanting to go back to Kentucky, but the Ohio River isn't safe since Indians are on the warpath there. Sure wish I could find somebody to go with me to find the way through the mountains. I'd give up this peddling in a wink."

Daniel's mind was made up before he went to

sleep that night. He would go with Finley, on a "long hunt" across the mountains in Kentucky.

"Wait for me, John, while I tend to a few matters," he said the next morning. "Stay on with us a few days, and we'll go to Kentucky together."

John Finley saw the old light burning in Daniel's eyes, the light he had seen as they sat around the wagoners' campfire long ago. He went out to the stable and hung his pack of pots and pans on the wall. He'd sold the best thing in the pack, his pack of dreams.

BOONE'S LONG HUNT, BIG TROUBLE

"James," Daniel Boone said to his oldest son, "you are almost a man now. I'll count on you to see that the corn is tended while I'm gone. The other children will help you keep the crows from eating it, and when it ripens you know how to bring it in. You and Israel can hunt for rabbits and squirrels for the family until I get back."

James had hoped that he, too, might go on the "long hunt" with his father and Mr. Finley, but when he asked to go, Daniel said, "I'm going all the way to Kentucky, son. It may be a long time before I get back, and I'll want to know that your mother has you here to help her."

There was an errand to do before the hunt began. Daniel had to go to court in town because of some trouble over his land. John Finley and John Stuart, Daniel's brother-in-law, who decided to join them on the "long hunt," went along.

Lawyer Richard Henderson helped Daniel settle his business in court. The three frontiersmen went back to his office to talk awhile before they headed back home.

"We're going to Kentucky, Judge," Boone told the lawyer. "Finley knows where there's plenty of good hunting there."

Lawyer Henderson listened closely, for he, too, had heard the stories of the land called Kentucky. He, too, had a dream about that faraway land. But his dream was not of hunting. He dreamed of beginning a colony there, and perhaps of being the governor of the new colony. His dream grew stronger as the men talked of that paradise over the mountains. The time had not yet come, but someday . . .

"Come and tell me of all you saw when you return, Daniel," he said as he shook hands. "Good luck on your long hunt!"

On the way home, the men called at the cabin of Daniel's brother, Squire Boone. Squire invited them to stay for the night, and again John Finley told of the wonders of Kentucky. It was easy to see that "Kentucky fever" was spreading to Squire.

"Tell you what, Dan'l," he said. "I can't get away now, but I'll join you out there. I'll wait until the

crops are in, and then head west with supplies for the winter."

On the first day of May, 1769, six men rode west from Daniel Boone's cabin. Boone, Finley and Stuart planned to spend all their time fur-hunting. The three other men would be the "camp-keepers." These men would get meat for their food, do the cooking and take care of the furs and skins the three hunters brought back to the camp.

As they headed west, Finley asked Boone, "Do you know of the Warriors' Path which leads to a pass through the Cumberland Mountains?"

"I've heard tell of it," Daniel said. "We'll find it."

It was not hard to find, for a "hunter's trace" had, by this time, made clear the path which Dr. Walker had followed to Cumberland Gap.

As they drew near to the great wall of the Cumberland Mountains, the last "fence" between them and Kentucky, Daniel and his friends were surprised to hear the sound of axes against tree trunks.

"I thought we'd left the last settlement back in the Holston Valley," Daniel said. "Sounds like someone's building a cabin away out here."

Soon the men came to a little clearing along the trail. About twenty men were working there. A cabin was partly built, and some of the men were planting corn between the stumps of the trees that had been cut for logs. A man named Joseph Martin was in charge of the work.

"Dr. Thomas Walker sent us out to take up his claim on this land," Martin said. He invited the hunters to stay and join the men as settlers.

"No, thank you," said Daniel. "We are off on a long hunt in Kentucky."

They stayed the night with the men and then moved on the last few miles to Cumberland Gap. In years to come, *Martin's Station* would be a welcome stopping place for other settlers going west.

The Warriors' Path was well worn and much more traveled than when Gabe Arthur had followed it many years before. Many hunters had gone through the pass in the mountains, but most of them soon turned west and southwest into the Tennessee River country. These six men followed the Warriors' Path northward into Kentucky.

When they had been traveling for five weeks, John Finley said, "We should be near the spot where I had my trading post. There should be an old Indian village not far from here. When we find it, we'll be in the best hunting grounds you ever could wish to see."

The weather had been rainy, and the men were tired of traveling.

"Why not make our camp here?" Daniel asked. "We can go out on our hunting trips from here, and come back to this as our station camp."

So *Station Camp* was built. It was just a shelter of poles and brush, but the men had a roof over their heads after five weeks in the open. The men would go out by ones or twos into the woods and bring their furs back to this place every few weeks.

Daniel Boone wanted to see what was beyond the next hills. He left the others one day to climb to the highest place between the Rockcastle River and the Kentucky River. From there he could see to the northwest for many, many miles.

"Beautiful, beautiful country," he said as he looked over the rolling land ahead. From that moment on, he knew that he must someday live here in Kentucky.

Finley, too, went off alone. When he came back

he said, "I found the old village where I traded, but no Indians live there now. The houses were burned."

"I'm glad to know that we don't have close neighbors," John Stuart said. "I wake up at night thinking the Indians are attacking, even though we haven't seen any."

The hunting began, and it was as Finley had promised. There seemed to be no end to the deer, the elk and the buffalo. The men set their traps in the fast-running streams, and each day there were beavers in them. The piles of skins and furs grew high.

Time and again the men went out from Station Camp, farther and farther into the wilderness. They set up small camps away from their main camp, where they kept their furs until they had time to take them back to Station Camp. Often they left the small camps unguarded, for still they had seen no Indians.

"We'll all be rich!" John Finley said. "We'll have to take our furs east soon, or our horses won't be able to carry them all."

Daniel Boone was having the time of his life. "I'm not going back yet. Squire will be here soon with supplies, and he won't go back without a hunt."

December came, and Squire had not come. The men stopped worrying about Indian attacks, for they had been told that the Indians stayed in their villages in the winter months. They did not know that word of the "long hunt" had carried along the Warriors' Path.

John Stuart and Daniel Boone had no idea that danger was near one day when they were following a buffalo trace together. They came to a place near a river where tall canes grew.

"They broke through these canes to get to the river, and not very long ago," John said.

"I'd sure like to get a really fine buffalo robe to send home to Rebecca," Daniel said. "Let's sneak up on them. They may still be drinking at the river."

It was hard to move quietly through the dry cane, but Daniel and John had learned how to do it in the past months. They saw the buffaloes without having been heard by the big, shaggy animals.

"A little closer, before we shoot," Daniel said.

But suddenly the buffaloes lifted their big heads, stood still for a moment, then splashed on through the river. They thundered away on the other side.

"Now how did they get wind of us when we are downwind from them?" Daniel asked. "There goes my fine bull, leading the herd."

He had the answer in a moment, for there was a sudden wild shriek and the sound of men crashing through the canes. Each hunter felt a strong arm around his throat as his own arms were pinned behind him. The shrieking grew louder, and in a moment twenty Indian braves circled about them. There was no chance for escape.

"We're in for it, John," Daniel said. But to his surprise, the leader of the Indian party ordered the braves to let go of the hunters. He was "Captain Will," an Indian who had been with white traders enough to learn to speak English.

"We watch you. We know you have many furs," Captain Will said to John and Daniel.

"We don't—" Daniel began, but Captain Will reached for his knife with one hand and Daniel's long brown hair with the other.

"Show us furs."

Daniel shrugged his shoulders. There was nothing to do but to lead the Indians to one of the small camps. He and John made as much noise as they could as they walked along, followed by the band of Indians riding horseback.

"If the camp-keeper has any sense, he'll run for it," Daniel thought. And that is just what happened. The Indians laughed as they packed the small piles of furs onto their horses and took the ammunition they found in the camp.

"That's all," Daniel said.

"Oh, no," said Captain Will. "We know. You have many camps, many furs. Go to next one now."

So off they went, toward the next camp. As soon as he had a chance to speak to John alone, Daniel said "By the time we get to Station Camp, all four of the others should have the furs packed onto the horses and be well on their way south."

They went to each of the small camps, circling far from Station Camp. When the last had been cleared of furs and ammunition, Captain Will said, "Now to big camp."

Daniel tried to stall for time. "What big camp?" he asked.

Captain Will said, "You know what big camp, Widemouth. Big camp by Warriors' Path. We see you come there. Seven moons go by, and you not go away. You take Indians' furs. Now you lose all of them."

Surely, by this time, Finley and the camp-keepers would have emptied Station Camp. Hopefully, Boone headed towards it.

His heart sank when they reached the camp. There were the many piles of furs, all in the bundles ready to be taken back east. There was no sign of the other four men who had run into the woods to hide.

The Indians took all of the furs as well as the last of the hunters' ammunition, the extra rifles and the horses. They took everything.

"Now, Widemouth," Captain Will said to Boone, "you see what happens when the white man kills the Indians' animals. We take back what is ours."

He made Boone and Stuart go north with him for three days' march. Then he ordered new moccasins and a rifle given to each prisoner. He also gave them each a piece of doeskin for "patch-leather," and enough powder and shot to kill small game for food on their way home.

"Now, brothers, go home," he said. "Don't come

back. Stay out of Indians' hunting grounds. Big trouble for you if you come back."

To their surprise, Boone and Stuart found themselves free. Captain Will held out his hand to each man, and then waited to see them start southward. They walked away.

"Let's make tracks fast," Stuart said. "I can still feel a scalping knife running around my head."

Daniel said, "And give up our horses? No, sir! We'll not go far. Tonight we'll go back to their camp and get some of our horses back."

Nothing Stuart said could make Daniel change his mind. That night, they crept up to the camp and made off with four horses. They rode until dawn, and then stopped to let the horses eat and drink.

John was bending over to tie the leather cord which held his moccasins in place when he heard a rumble.

"Grab the horses, Dan'l" he shouted. "They're coming!"

But the Indians were upon them before they could jump onto their horses.

"So!" cried Captain Will. "You will steal horses!"

"They were our horses!" Daniel cried.

Captain Will pulled the bells from around two of the horse's necks and hung one around Daniel's neck and one around John's.

"Dance! Make the bells ring!" he cried. Daniel and John had no choice. They danced. The Indians laughed with glee.

"This time you go with us a longer way, until we cross Ohio River," Captain Will told them. He knew that the horses could not easily be brought back across the river.

But a few nights later, Stuart and Boone again had a chance to escape. This time they hid in the tall cane until the Indians gave up looking for them and went on their way. But there was no chance to get their horses, so the two men headed south on foot. A few days later, they were at Station Camp. Not a man was in sight, nor a scrap of food.

"They've given us up for lost and gone back home," Daniel said.

"We'd better do the same," John said. "I have a feeling that Captain Will won't be so kind if he catches us again."

But Daniel was not ready to give up. "With nothing to show for our time here? Not old Dan'l Boone!"

"What will we use for ammunition?" John asked.

Even Daniel did not have a ready answer for that question. And a moment later, he and John both wished they had hurried on, too. They heard a crackling twig, and caught sight of a brown figure as it slipped behind a tree not far off.

Without a word, Daniel and John took shelter behind trees, and got their rifles ready to fire. The moments went by and there was not a sound in the winter woods. The heavy silence was broken by the harsh cry of a blue jay. Then the woods were quiet again. Daniel peered from behind his tree, just as the unknown man did.

"If I didn't know better, I'd swear that was a white face I saw," Daniel said. Then a sudden thought came to him. Could it be his brother, Squire, here at last with supplies?

"White men and friends!" he called. "Show yourself!"

A moment later, Squire Boone was shaking Daniel's hand. A second man was coming from farther away, leading several horses.

"I promised I'd come, Dan'l," Squire said. "And I've got plenty of supplies for a winter's hunt. When do we begin?"

Daniel Boone knew then that the Kentucky woods would be his home for months to come.

BOONE STOPPED BY INDIANS

Soon after Squire reached the meeting place, John Stuart went into the woods to hunt alone. Weeks passed, and he did not return.

"The Indians got him," said the man who had come with Squire. "I'm going home now, while I still have two legs to carry me."

So Daniel and Squire were left alone in the great wilderness. Often, Daniel thought of what Captain Will had told him, but it did not frighten him. It only made him a little more careful.

"We'll set up our main camp away from the Warriors' Path this time," he told Squire. "And we'd better take care to hide ourselves as much as we can. I hope to get home to see that new son of mine some day, and I plan to keep out of Captain Will's path.

Squire Boone had brought news of the birth of Daniel Morgan Boone in December, while the baby's father was in Kentucky.

"Rebecca misses you, Daniel," Squire said.

For a moment, Daniel pictured himself riding up to the cabin in the Yadkin Valley. His horses would be loaded with packs of furs which would buy all the things his family wanted.

But he had almost no furs.

"Can't go home until I have something to show for my time and my work," he said, and cleaned up his rifle for the next day's hunt.

The two brothers set their traps for beaver and otter in the fast-running streams. Day after day, they watched for deer, elk and buffalo. The winter ended and spring began. The pile of furs grew high again. May came, and Daniel had been away from home for a whole year.

"Ammunition's low, Daniel," Squire said then. "We have a good pack of furs ready. Let's go home."

But even then, Daniel was not ready to go. As spring came on, his dream of bringing his family to live in Kentucky had grown stronger. He would find a good home place while Squire made a trip back to the Yadkin.

"You go, Squire. Bring back more supplies. And tell Rebecca I'm going to find us a new home place."

So Squire loaded all the horses but one with furs.

He rode that one, and left Daniel alone in the woods.

"We'll meet as soon as I can get the supplies and get back here," Squire said. "Late July, likely."

Daniel set out on foot to do what he had long wanted to do. He headed northwest to see the bluegrass country, and as he walked, his love for Kentucky grew. When, later in the summer, he met Squire again, he had found the place where he wanted to begin a settlement.

The two men hunted and trapped all winter long, never staying long enough in one place for the Indians to find them. In March of 1771, even Daniel was ready to head for home. He had been away almost two years. The brothers had a good pack of furs, and Daniel knew more about Kentucky than any man alive.

"I'll use my share of the money to buy supplies and bring Rebecca back here with me," he said.

But before they had gone far along the Warriors' Path, they met a party of Indians. When they had moved on, Squire and Daniel were lucky to be alive and free. But they had not a single fur to take back to Yadkin.

It was a sad Daniel who reached home. He was

too poor to buy the things he would need to take his family to Kentucky, but he could not settle down to life in the Yadkin Valley again. He moved to the Holston Valley, a step nearer to Kentucky.

The Kentucky dream burned inside him. In 1773, he went to see his old friend, Lawyer Richard Henderson, now a judge. He talked to the judge about beginning a Kentucky settlement.

"I would like to get started on it, but I can't do it right now," Judge Henderson said. "Beginning a new colony takes careful planning, Daniel. Planning, and money, too, for we must first buy the land from the Indians if we expect them to let us live there in peace."

Daniel was disappointed. He went back home.

"The best land will all be taken by the time Judge Henderson is ready," he thought to himself, for word had reached him of other exploring parties going to Kentucky. "I'll go without him."

On the way back to the Holston, he talked to the people he met about how fine it would be to get away from high taxes and live in beautiful Kentucky. In the Yadkin Valley, he stopped to visit his wife's relatives, the Bryans, and found good listeners in their cabin.

"We'll go, if it's such a wonderful place," the Bryans said. Daniel was delighted. Plans were made before he went on home.

"Rebecca! Pack up a few things. We're going to Kentucky to live!" he cried as reached his cabin.

Rebecca stared at her husband. She picked up little Jesse Bryan Boone, who was just three months old. There were eight young Boones now, from sixteen-year-old James down to baby Jesse. Susannah, the oldest girl, was thirteen, and planning her wedding to Will Hays, for frontier girls often married when they were in their early teens. It hardly seemed the right time to take off for Kentucky. Rebecca didn't hear all that Daniel was saying. She only knew that if she said "no" he would go without her.

"Yes, Daniel," she said at last. "I'll start packing."

They left on a September day, with all the horses they could gather to carry their goods over the trail through the wilderness, and a few head of cattle. There were forty people in all. Ten of them were Daniel's own family. There was Squire Boone and his family, the Bryans, a neighbor and his family and a few men without families who were going for the adventure and the hunting.

Traveling was easy at first, until the pioneers left the well-traveled part of the trail. The summer's growth had crowded in on the Warriors' Path when they reached it, and branches clawed at the packs on the horses' backs. They scratched the arms and faces of those who walked, and tore at the women's skirts.

Sometimes a horse's pack would touch a yellow jacket nest. Then, horses, cattle and people would be scattered through the woods for an hour afterward.

The travelers crossed two of the mountain ranges which lay between the Holston Valley and Kentucky and only the Cumberland Ridge blocked their way. Cumberland Gap was not far ahead, not more than one day's travel.

Daniel looked about at the faces of his little band of followers as they gathered around the campfires at the end of the day. He was worried about the supplies they had with them. Martin's Station, where he had hoped to buy more food, had been passed that day. But Joseph Martin had found the Indians too unfriendly in the past years, and his cabins stood empty.

"Should we turn back, Daniel?" Squire asked.

"Turn back? Of course not," Daniel said. "But we will need more flour. I'll send James back to Captain Russell's place and ask him to bring more flour with him when he comes. He may be ready to start for Kentucky now, and he can ride back with James."

Captain Russell and his family owned one of the frontier posts farthest west. Daniel had talked with him as the pioneers stopped to rest at his place, and the Kentucky dream had spread to Captain Russell, too.

"I'll need a few days to get ready," the captain said, "but I'll follow soon with my family and several extra men."

James left the camp in the morning and rode back toward Captain Russell's post. He reached the post safely, and soon was starting west again. With him rode the captain's son, Henry, who was about James' own age, two negro slaves and two workmen. They led several pack horses loaded with supplies.

"I'll be able to start out in about two days," Captain Russell had said as they left. "Just go ahead with Daniel Boone, and choose a good home place for us, Henry."

Henry and James were enjoying their adventure. Although James had often been in the wilderness with his father, he had not learned to read the trail signs as well as Daniel could, and accidentally he led the group off the main trail. When he found it again, he was not sure of where they were, or how far from the place where Daniel and the others waited.

They came to a good camping place on a creek bank late in the day.

"We had better camp here for the night," James decided. He did not know that his father was only three miles ahead, and that the little group could have made it to the main camp that night.

After supper, James, Henry and the others spread out their blankets around the dying campfire, and settled down for the night. As James lay there waiting for sleep to come, it seemed to him that the wolves were howling more than usual, and too near the camp. He listened uneasily to the calls. They began much as a big dog's bark, but changed into a howl as the pitch rose higher and higher. James shivered.

Henry, rolled in his blanket beside James, asked, "Why are the wolves howling so much tonight, James? They sound different tonight. Kind of scares me."

One of the men said, "Seems as if they're all around us. Makes me shiver."

A man named Isaac Crabtree laughed. He had been over the mountains before and liked to seem braver than the others. "You'll be shivering worse when we get to Kentucky. The buffalo will be bellowing in your ears along with the wolves and the wildcats. Better get used to it and go to sleep."

But Henry Russell could not get to sleep. He said, "Those howls answer each other. They come first from one side and then the other. It could be Indians, and not wolves at all. We better place a guard."

"There are friendly Indians along this part of the trail," James said. "No need to worry. The Indians are glad to find traders any time, and they wouldn't hurt us if they found us here. Let's go to sleep and get an early start in the morning. Likely we'll catch up with Father tomorrow."

The campers were quiet then. The horses moved about restlessly, their jingling bells telling of their movements. A wildcat's howl joined that of the wolves and an owl cried sadly. But the journey had been long and hard, and the boys and men were tired. Sleep came in spite of the forest sounds.

James opened his eyes to a sky gray with dawn. He was about to sit up and awaken the others when he heard the sound of running moccasined feet.

"Look out!" he cried. But it was too late. The camp was suddenly alive with flying arrows. Each man jumped up and tried to escape to the woods or the creek.

James felt the sharp pain of an arrow in his back just as he saw Henry fall to the ground. James wheeled about and saw an Indian heading toward him. A second arrow struck his body, but even through his pain James knew that the Indian was one who had been in his father's cabin on the Yadkin and had eaten at the table with the Boone family.

"Big Jim! Don't you know me? It's James Boone!" he cried out. But Big Jim said nothing. One of the two negro slaves, hiding in a pile of driftwood in the creek, saw the Indian bring his tomahawk down onto James' head. He saw the Indians kill Henry and one of the workmen, too. Isaac Crabtree escaped into the woods. The other slave, screaming with pain, was carried away with the Indians when they finally left.

Later that day, Captain Russell and his men came along the trail, having started a little sooner than they had planned. The slave, trembling and sick, came from his hiding place as Captain Russell saw the horrible sight.

"Ride ahead to warn the Boones," Captain Russell said, and one of his men hurried on. Captain Russell's heart was heavy as he began the work of digging graves.

The adventure of riding to new Kentucky homes was over. Daniel never gave up looking for Big Jim, who had so badly treated the Boones in return for friendship. Twenty-four years later, he faced the big Indian and Big Jim gave his life as he had taken that of James Boone.

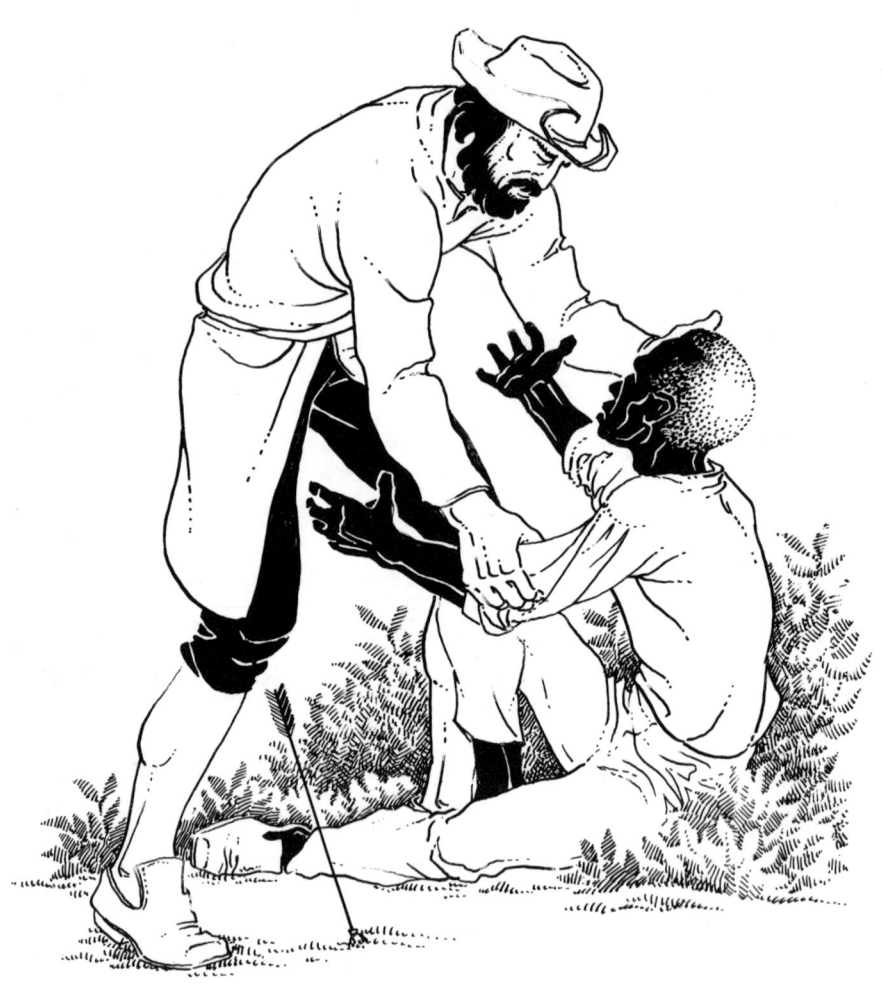

The pioneers turned back, sick at heart. Daniel, alone, had wanted to go on. The dream of Kentucky was so strong in him that it could not be killed.

WILDERNESS ROAD

A year and a half after that sad day on the Warriors' Path, the fire of a council burned brightly in the eastern Tennessee hills. Indians and white men sat around the fire, listening to the words of Judge Richard Henderson.

Henderson finished his talk and sat down. An Indian stood up to say in the Cherokee tongue all that Henderson had said in English. His words still hung in the cold air of the March night when a young Indian, called *Dragging Canoe* by the white men, jumped to his feet. His eyes burned with more than the light of the fire as he spoke.

"Whole nations have melted away, like balls of snow before the sun," he said, and his voice rang with feeling. "The whites have crossed the Great Salt Sea and built homes on our land. Broad rivers and deep forests did not stop them, and we, the people who own the land, have been swept from their way like leaves before a wind. Now they would cross the mountains, to build their homes in our hunting grounds.

"We must move on again, to a more distant wilderness. Should we, my brothers, sell more of our land so that we may be driven even farther? No, I say! That may be all right for old men, men too old to hunt or fight. As for me, my young warriors and I will stand firm to hold our hunting grounds forever."

The men seated about the council fire stirred uneasily.

The interpreter's voice, giving Dragging Canoe's speech in English, caught a little of the anger of the young chief. Dragging Canoe's father, Little Carpenter, was offering to sell thousands of acres of Kentucky land to Judge Richard Henderson and his partners for a pile of knives and guns, bright-colored cloth, copper and iron kettles and other of the white man's goods.

When the interpreter had finished, Judge Henderson arose again. He was a tall man, broad and strong, and all eyes around the circle turned to him. He spoke in a voice that was strong and at the same time quiet.

"Brother," he said, "we are here to do good for

each other. We are not here to draw the sword of anger, but to smoke the pipe of peace together. Let us gather around the feast table as friends. We shall go on with our talks tomorrow."

Daniel Boone, sitting with the other white men in the circle, listened to the strong voice of his old friend. He saw the older chiefs' eyes turn with longing to the great pile of trading goods. Daniel was sure that the judge would manage Dragging Canoe well, and that the older chiefs would put their marks on the treaty.

Soon they would be on their way to Kentucky again. Judge Henderson had talked to many Indians in the last year, and had decided that the land he wanted belonged to the Cherokees. He would pay them for it, and then a group of pioneers would go in safety to *Transylvania,* as he had named the new colony. The name meant *across the woodlands,* and across the woodlands to the blue-grass country that Daniel loved they soon would be going. If Dragging Canoe did not make trouble—

Daniel, Judge Henderson and his partners moved about among the chiefs as the great roasts of pork and beef were served. They spoke of the great pile of trading goods, asking the chiefs what they most wanted and if they had enough horses to carry so much away with them. There were no more words of anger before all the people had gone to their tents for the night.

The next morning, the council was called again. Dragging Canoe made another angry speech, but no other chiefs came to stand by his side when he called for those who would stand with him.

Judge Henderson read the treaty aloud. Then, one by one, all the chiefs but Dragging Canoe made their mark on the paper.

The young chief's eyes burned with hatred as he watched the signing of the treaty. He turned to Daniel Boone and spoke. His voice was low, but his words rang in Daniel's mind, and his memory called them back many times in the years that followed.

"You have bought a land of sunshine," Dragging Canoe said, "but from here on a cloud shall hang over it. You may build your settlement, but it shall be on ground which is dark and bloody."

Henderson called the chiefs together again. "Brothers, I have more gifts for you. I have long rifles and the powder and shot which will make your hunting easy. To go to Kentucky, we must walk on the land of our brothers, the Cherokees, and we do not want to do that. We would buy from you a roadway to Kentucky."

Dragging Canoe jumped to his feet again. "Have you not taken enough from my people? Must you have more, and then more again?" Anger made his voice sharp. He looked about at his fellow chiefs, but their eyes turned away from his. No voices rose to join his.

The young chief turned on his heel and walked away from the council as his brothers ate again of the white man's food.

"Daniel," Henderson said a little later. "This part of the treaty is sure to go through now that Dragging Canoe is gone. You go ahead and get the trail ready. When you get to Otter Creek, begin the work of cabin building."

The plans had all been made ahead of time. Henderson had a map of Kentucky, and on it was marked the place where Otter Creek empties into the Kentucky River. There, on the very spot where Daniel had so long dreamed of building his cabin, the new colony was to have its beginning. He hurried from the council to join the thirty men who were to help him widen the trail to Kentucky. They were to meet him where Kingsport, Tennessee, is today. Each of the thirty was a frontiersman who knew how to swing an axe and to hunt.

Each man's pay would be a piece of land in the new settlement. Daniel himself was to have 20,000 acres.

As he rode his horse toward the place where he was to meet the men, Daniel pictured himself as master of all that land. He saw waving fields of blue grass, a deep-running river fed by sparkling streams, and woods alive with elk and deer. He saw a herd of buffalo crossing the blue grass to a stream and himself aiming his rifle at the big bull who led the herd.

"Kentucky!" he said aloud, and the name was music to his ears. If only Rebecca could be happy about it, too!

It was the tenth day of March, 1775, as Daniel led his axmen to the work of marking the trail over the mountains so clearly that all could follow it who chose to do so. Each day, the men swung their axes to clear away the brush that hung over the trail.

They marked trees along the way with blazes, following the worn paths where buffalo hoofs and Indian moccasins had shown the white hunters the easiest way.

The *Wilderness Road*, as they called the widened trail, went through the valley where Ambrose Powell had left his name on so many beech trees. There it swung southwest for twenty miles or so. On the right towered the high wall of the Cumberlands. Ahead a short way was the Warriors' Path and Cumberland Gap. Boone's men, marking the big trees and chopping away young ones, heard the sound of axes other than their own.

"Now who could that be?" Daniel asked, and rode ahead to find out. He found a party of men working at rebuilding the cabins which Captain Joseph Martin had been building when Daniel Boone passed that way in 1769. Captain Martin himself was there.

"Hello!" called Daniel, and soon the men were exchanging news of what had happened in the years gone by.

"Cherokees got too bad, and we had to leave before winter," Joseph Martin explained. Then

Daniel told him about the treaty with the Cherokees to let them use the trail and widen it.

"Judge Henderson will be coming this way soon with more men for Kentucky," Daniel told him. "When we have some cabins ready, we shall bring our families. It will be wonderful to live where there is plenty of elbow room!"

The men spent the night at Martin's Station, and then were on their way again. Little widening was needed on the well-worn trail through Cumberland Gap. The Warriors' Path took them to Cumberland River and the river crossing where the water was not too deep for horses to walk through. Eight miles farther, they left the main Indian road and followed a hunter's path. There was more ax work to do there, through the hilly, brushy woodland.

"The woods close in on a path too fast," Daniel said as he chopped out year-old trees growing on the path. "But from now on, there will be so many people following this trail to Kentucky that the road will stay open."

At a place called *Hazel Patch*, Daniel led the ax-men northward toward the more open country. They had been on their way ten days when they came to Big Hill, at the edge of the mountains. There Daniel had stood at the beginning of his Long Hunt. There he had first seen the rolling land that had been in his dreams ever since.

"There it is, boys," he said. "There's that beautiful bluegrass country we've been telling you about."

All the men stopped to look at the grasslands that reached farther than their eyes could see. Patches of woods and dark ribbons of trees along the streams made it seem a real paradise.

William Hays, who had just been married to Daniel's oldest daughter, Susannah, took a deep breath and said, "Smell that sweet clover! It's the land of milk and honey, for sure!"

With only fifteen miles to go, it was a happy group of men who rolled themselves into their blankets to sleep that night. They were sound asleep almost as soon as they closed their eyes, for the work of chopping out young trees and cane was very tiring. Every man was still sound asleep an hour before dawn when trouble came creeping through the woods.

"Indians!" one of the men yelled as rifle fire sounded.

It seemed as if the shots came from all directions. As the men ran for the woods, Indians moved in toward the glowing ashes of their campfire, swinging tomahawks and yelling.

One of the men, Captain William Twitty, had set up a tent for himself, and in it his bulldog slept by his side. The tent stood out in the darkness and several Indians fired into it. The captain cried out in pain.

He could not run, for shots had hit him in both his knees. He heard the wild cry of a Shawnee brave as the Indian ripped the tent away. Captain Twitty tried to crawl away, but the Indian did not mean to let him go. He raised his tomahawk, but Captain Twitty's bulldog jumped for his throat. The Indian fell, screaming.

A second Indian struck out at the dog with a tomahawk, and the animal fell back. The dog moved no more, but he had given his master time to drag himself into the darkness away from the glowing ashes of the fire. Daniel Boone and the other men who had been able to pick up their rifles began to fire from behind the trees. The Indians, with one last wild cry, ran back to where they had left their horses.

No one slept in that last hour of darkness. One by one, the men crept back to their camp to wait for dawn. One man was badly wounded in the hip. Captain Twitty's servant, sleeping just outside the tent, had been hit in the first round of fire and was dead. Yesterday's joy was dead, too, as daylight came.

"We can't go on today," Daniel told the men. "Captain Twitty and Felix Walker are too badly hurt. We'll have to build a shelter for them to stay in until they are well enough to travel."

Daniel looked about for a good spot off the trail a little way. Soon he and the other men were cutting logs to make a tiny roofless "fort" in which the men could stay. They carried the two wounded men to the shelter and tried to make them comfortable.

"I'll be back soon," Daniel said then, and headed off into the woods. He was gone for an hour or two, and when he came back he had some plants and roots he had dug in the woods. From these he made medicine to help heal the wounds.

In spite of all the men could do for him, Captain

Twitty grew weaker. He died after two days, but the medicines helped Felix Walker, and he was a little better each day.

The day after Captain Twitty died, a few of the men went hunting to get food for the camp. They were a mile or two from the little "fort" when they heard a call.

"Did you hear that?" Daniel asked. "It sounded like a boy's voice."

They listened and called an answer when they heard the voice again. A few minutes later, a white boy came towards them.

"Can you help me?" he called out. "Indians came to my father's camp last night. I ran to the woods to hide and I'm afraid to go back alone."

"We'll help you, boy," Daniel said. He sent the other men back to the "fort" while he and Squire Boone went with the boy. They found the camp. The boy's father and another man were digging graves for two others. The Shawnees had taken this camp by surprise, too. The fact that the Cherokees had sold the land to the white men meant nothing at all to them, for they thought of Kentucky as their own hunting grounds.

The boy's father said, "We're with James Harrod. We came down the Ohio River by canoe this spring, and then up the Kentucky River to the place where James Harrod's new settlement is. Do you know the place?"

"I do," said Daniel. "Another fellow and I were sent there last year when Harrod first came to Kentucky. We warned them that the Indians were on the warpath, and they left. Do you mean they've come back again?"

"We do," the men said, "and we've come to stay."

Daniel Boone was a little disappointed to learn that another settlement had begun before his. But, he thought, the settlements could help each other, and there was plenty of room in Kentucky.

"If you need help, come to the place where Otter Creek empties into the Kentucky," he told the men as he and Squire left. "We'll be building a good fort there, and Judge Henderson will be with us soon with plenty of men."

The Indians were not seen again in the week that followed. Felix Walker grew strong enough to be moved, and the men cut the trail the last fifteen miles. They made a stretcher with two poles and a blanket and hung it between two horses, one walking behind the other. Felix rode in it up the narrow trail to the place where Boonesborough soon would be built.

As the men drew near, they saw a herd of buffalo running through a field of bluegrass along the river's edge, frightened away by the men's coming. It could have been the herd of Daniel's daydream.

"We'll have plenty to eat," Daniel said happily. This was home, the end of the trail to the wilderness.

Many a settler was to travel the Wilderness Road and the other trails to the land beyond the mountains in the next years. True, they were troubled years at first, and Dragging Canoe's threat of a "dark and bloody ground" came to be too real.

But courage lived on in the wilderness. It was the same kind of courage that was in the hearts of the men who set out from Fort Henry so many years ago. With its help, the trails became roads and roads became highways. The wilderness was tamed.

THE END

Edith McCall, in her *Frontiers of America* books, writes in simple, uncluttered text without losing the dramatic impact of her true stories of real people.

Her purpose is to make these stories of our country available to younger readers and still vital and interesting to a wide age range. Mrs. McCall now lives in the Ozarks and writes for children. For many years, she was a reading consultant in LaGrange, Illinois.

Fort Loudoun Regional Library
718 George St.
Athens, Tenn. 37303

Cumberland Gap and trails West 29790
McCall, Edith
973.2 McC
Rockwood Public Library
YA

DISCARD